Maths Age 6–7

Sue Atkinson

Sue Atkinson has many years' experience as a primary school teacher and as a lecturer in maths education. She has also done research into how children learn maths. She is now a freelance maths consultant working with children, teachers and parents throughout the UK and internationally. She has two grown-up children and a young grandson.

Consultant: Shirley Clarke

Shirley Clarke works at the Institute of Education, University of London. She has been a primary school teacher and a maths advisor and was involved in developing the first SATs. She is the author of many maths books for teachers, children and parents.

Illustrated by **Linzi Henry**

About this book

This book contains number activities suitable for 6- and 7-year-olds. They are based on the National Curriculum and National Numeracy requirements for Year 2.

The activities gradually become more demanding, so it is important to start at the beginning.

The numeracy skills taught or practised in each unit are stated at the top of the page. A note at the foot of the page tells you more about the purpose of the activities and gives advice about how to help your child with them.

'Superstar' stickers are included to help motivate children. There is a space for your child to stick a star when he or she has completed a unit. The 'See what I can do' page at the back of the book has space for another star, and is intended to give your child a sense of achievement, while providing you with a useful checklist of skills.

Each unit ends with a positive comment. Encouragement from you will work wonders, so be generous with your praise!

There are 100 Buzzy Bees hidden in the book for your child to discover.

Hodder Children's Books
a division of
Hodder Headline Limited

How to help your child

- Find a quiet place to work, preferably sitting at a table.
- Work with your child little and often, but don't insist if he or she is tired or happily doing something else. Help with reading the instructions where necessary.
- Let your child return to favourite pages once they have been completed, to play games, to do more counting or to talk about the activities.
- Encourage your child to check his or her work.
- Talk to your child about numbers when you are out shopping or laying the table, as well as during play. Try to do some counting together every day.
- You will need a spinner to play some of the games. You can easily make one from a pencil and a paperclip using the circle printed on the page. To make it work, flick the paperclip lightly with a finger to make it spin round the pencil tip.

- Small objects, such as pasta shapes, raisins or small toys, are useful for counting. For other activities, it will help to have coins or a tape measure handy.

Above all, be relaxed – and have fun!

Pirate island

Counting on

Hello! I'm Penny Parrot and I'm going to help you with your maths.

How many of these are there?

Help your child to 'count on' by holding one number in her head and counting on the next, e.g. *You have 8 apples, count on 10 more is 18*. If she tries to count from 1 each time (rather than from the number in her head), you will need to repeat the concept using easy numbers, e.g. *Put out 3 spoons and 4 more spoons – that is 4, 5, 6, 7 altogether.*

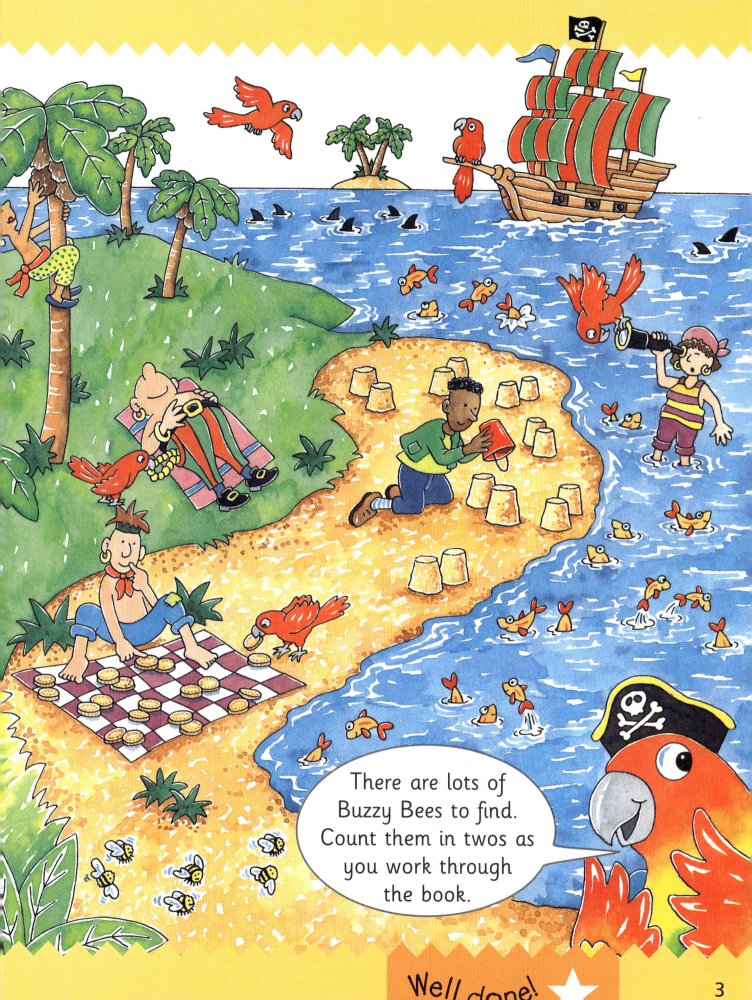

Describing and extending number sequences

Number patterns

Continue these patterns.

1. 0 3 6 9 __ __ __ __

2. 0 5 10 15 __ __ __ __

Now fill in the missing numbers.

3. 2 4 __ __ __ __ 14 __ __ 20

*Which are the **odd** numbers? Which are the **even** numbers?*

4. 9 __ 13 15 __ 19

5. 1 2 __ 8 16 __ 64

What is happening to the numbers in question 5?

6. Now make up a number pattern of your own.

> Recognising number patterns will help your child learn his times tables by heart, and will speed up his arithmetic.

Wonderful!

Ordering numbers

Football shirts

Put the numbers on the shirts in order, from the smallest to the largest.

① 10 7
   8 12

② 28 17 68
   86 24 39

Now put these numbers on the number lines in order, from the smallest to the largest.

③ 21 71 14
   96 17 12

④ 13 31 64
   96 17 12

This time, order them starting from the largest number down to the smallest.

Ask questions such as
Is 87 more or less than 45?
Which is larger, 17 or 71?

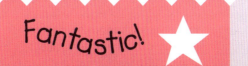

5

Positioning numbers on a number line

Number lines

Number lines don't always go up in ones.

Fill in the missing numbers.

1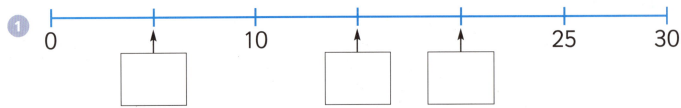

These number lines go up in tens and fives.

2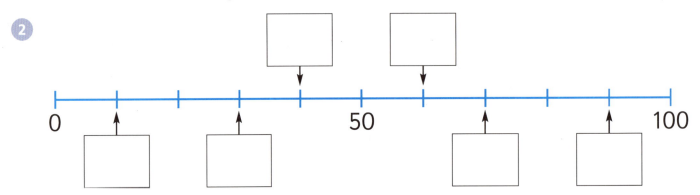

3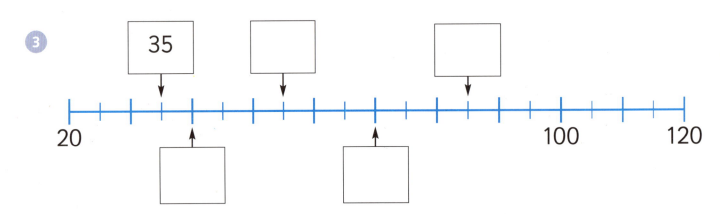

Mark these numbers on the line: 20 40 65 75

4

Number lines are very important in helping your child to be good at maths. She could make one from 0 to 100 and put it up in the kitchen for easy reference.

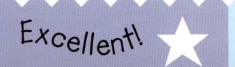

6

Positioning numbers on a hundred square

Where does it go?

Be careful! This is quite hard.

① Look at the hundred square.
Fill in these numbers: 64 99 51 40 13 85

1	2	3	4	5	6	7	8	9	10
11	12								
								100

② Now fill in the rest of the numbers to check if you filled in question 1 correctly.

Use the complete hundred square to add 10.

③ 20 — 10 more is ☐

④ 70 — 10 more is ☐

⑤ 85 — 10 more is ☐

⑥ 39 — 10 more is ☐

Help your child to count in threes, fours, fives and tens using the hundred square.

Brilliant!

7

Reading and writing numbers in figures and words

Penny Parrot's purses

Think carefully about the hundreds, tens and units.

Numbers can be written in different ways.
Join these purses to their matching number.

1

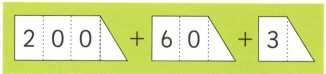

200 + 60 + 3

30 + 6

seventy-nine

three hundred

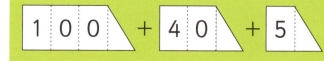

100 + 40 + 5

four hundred and eighty-seven

50 + 7

Split these numbers into hundreds, tens and units.

Can you write the numbers in words?

2 68 is [6 0] + [   ]   sixty..........................

3 39 is [   ] + [   ]   ....

4 46 is [   ] + [   ]   ....

It is likely that your child will find some of the spellings difficult. Point out that, surprisingly, there is no 'u' in 'forty'.

Good work!

Understanding place value

Robin Hood's target

There is 1 arrow in the hundreds, 2 in the tens and 3 in the units. What does that make?

1 What number is shown on this dartboard?

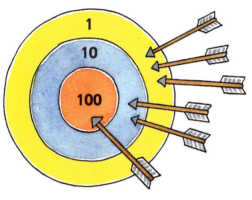

| 1 | 0 | 0 | + | | | + | | | = | | | |

2 Shoot six arrows of your own. Write your score.

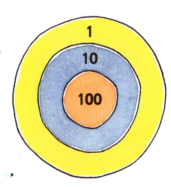

| | | | + | | | + | | | = | | | |

Here are some questions to think about.

3 The **largest** number you can make with six arrows is ....

4 The **smallest** number you can make is ....

You could make a family game like this by making a paper target. Place it on the floor and gently toss six pieces of dried pasta on to it to score.

Well done!

Telling number stories

By the pond

Read these number stories to a helper.

① **10** gnats and **10** more makes ☐ gnats.

    + =

② **20** tadpoles and **20** more makes ☐ tadpoles.

    20 + 20 = ☐

③ **15** flies and **1** disappears leaves ☐ flies.

    15 ◯ ☐ = ☐

④ **5** ladybirds and **5** more and another **5** makes ☐ ladybirds.

   5 + 5 + 5 = ☐

   or   5 × 3 = ☐

It is important that children see how maths applies in real situations. You could tell maths stories over meals, perhaps *I have 8 sausages to share between 4 people. How many sausages will we each get?*

Well counted!

Choosing the appropriate operation

Is it adding?

Circle the calculation which matches the number story.

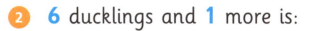
Read each story carefully!

① **11** swans and **3** fly away is:

11 + 3
11 − 3
11 ÷ 3

② **6** ducklings and **1** more is:

6 + 1
6 − 1
6 × 1

③ **18** gems in a bag and **1** falls out is:

18 − 1
18 × 1
18 + 1

④ **50** soldiers in the horse and **25** climb out is:

50 + 25
50 − 25
50 × 25

⑤ **3** blind mice and **13** more is: 3 + 13   3 − 13   3 ÷ 13

⑥ Now tell a story to go with 11 − 7.

Children can find choosing an appropriate operation surprisingly difficult, but it is an essential skill for them to learn. Talk about the page and the four operations (+, −, ÷ and ×) there are to choose from.

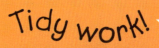

11

Adding two numbers

Addition tables

① This is how an addition square works.

+	5	8	10
2	7	10	12
3	⑧	11	

This is 5 add 3

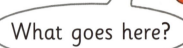

What goes here?

Now fill in the missing numbers.

②

+	2	3	4	5	6	7
2	4					
4						
6			10	11		
8						
10						17

③

+	5	8		7	
10			20		10
20			30		20
	30			36	25
	35			37	

You have to think hard how to do this one!

Help your child to think logically about Question 3. You could suggest trying to find the first missing number along the top after the 5 and 8. Say *10 add something is 20. What is the something? It is 10*. The first missing number in the vertical axis is the next easiest one to work out.

Subtracting one number from another

Subtraction stories

Finish these calculations.

① **20** balloons, then **2** pop leaving ☐

20 − 2 = ☐

② **20** jam tarts, but the knave of hearts steals **5** leaving ☐

20 − ☐ = ☐

③ **Now make up your own subtraction calculation.**

20 sweets, eat ☐ leaving ☐

20 − ☐ = ☐

④ **Draw your own take away story with 20.**

20 − ☐ = ☐

Now try these.

⑤ 17 − ☐ = 7   ⑥ 21 − ☐ = 13   ⑦ 27 − ☐ = 4

Here the maths is put in a story context to help your child to understand what subtraction means.

Well done!

Estimating

Guess how many

Estimate how many stars and snowflakes there are.

"Don't count them, just guess."

1

"That looks like more than 10 stars to me!"

I think there are about ☐ stars.

2

"I've circled 10 snowflakes to help you guess."

I think there are about ☐ snowflakes.

Count the stars and snowflakes. How close were your guesses?

> Estimating is a very important basic skill which will be used to make accurate and quick calculations in later years. You could extend the work to guessing how many pages are in a book or how many potatoes are in a bag, for instance.

Wonderful!

14

Rounding up and down

To round up or down, you need to look at the units number.

23 is nearer 20 than 30, so it **rounds down**.
27 is nearer 30 than 20, so it **rounds up**.
56 is nearer to 60 than 50, so it **rounds up**.

And numbers which end in 5 always round up!

So 55 is **rounded up** to 60.

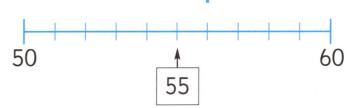

Round these numbers to the nearest 10.

1. 43 ☐   2. 27 ☐   3. 85 ☐   4. 58 ☐

Now circle the nearest 10.

5. 6 + 16 is nearest — 20 / 30 / 50

6. 49 − 8 is nearest — 10 / 40 / 50

Make up a sum with the answer nearest to 50.

7. ☐ ○ ☐ is nearest to 50.

Let your child look back to the hundred square on page 7 to make sure he understands the task. Number 7 is very hard!

Adding and subtracting money

Money game

| Buy a comic 25p  | You receive birthday money £1.50 | Dad gives you 50p | Buy sweets and spend 15p | You clean the windows. Mum gives you 25p |

Lose 10p

Gran gives you 20p

Start with £1.10

Add up the coins. How much is there altogether in each question?

①    = ☐

②   = ☐

③   = £ ☐ and ☐ p

Play the 'Money Game' in the border with some friends.

To play this game, you will need to use the spinner, and have some real money (if possible) and a counter for each player.

1. Start with £1.10 each and choose one player to look after the 'bank'.

2. Take turns to spin the spinner and move that many spaces. You either get money from the bank or give it to the bank.

3. The winner is the player with the LEAST amount of money when they get home! Note: Each player must explain what they are doing each time, e.g. *I've got to change my pound coin for smaller coins so that I can pay the bank 25p for the comic.*

| Spend £1 at the fair  | You win £2 in a short story competition  | Go to the zoo. Pay the 50p entrance fee  | Spend 20p in the zoo shop  | You get 35p pocket money  |

④   = £ ☐ and ☐ p

Uncle gives you 30p

⑤   = £ ☐ and ☐ p

Buy an apple for 10p

Buy crisps for 15p

⑥ **Now join the coins to the correct total amount.**

    £1.15

     £1.20

    £2.50

Well played! ★

Measuring with centimetres

How long are they?

Copy this ruler carefully onto spare paper, and cut it out.

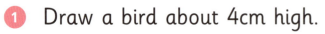

1. Draw a bird about 4cm high.

2. This flag is  cm deep.

 cm wide.

3. Peter Pan is 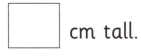 cm tall.

4. Captain Hook is  cm tall.

Supervise the copying and cutting out of the ruler, or use a real ruler or tape measure. Help your child to start measuring from 0 each time. Show her other rulers and tape measures.

Recognising and naming 3D shapes

Shapes at the grocer

1. **Join each shape to the correct name.**

  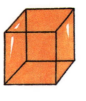  

sphere — cone   cylinder   cuboid   cube   pyramid

Now look at the shapes in this shop.

How many of each shape are there altogether?

2. spheres   3. cuboids   4. pyramids

5. cubes   6. cones   7. cylinders

Find boxes in the kitchen cupboard and see if your child can match them to pictures on this page.

Brilliant!

Reading a simple scale

Weighing and measuring

"This potato weighs 200 grams. What do the other things weigh?"

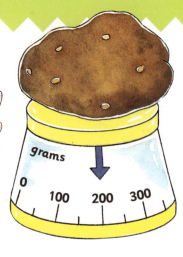

1 This mini-monster weighs ☐ grams.

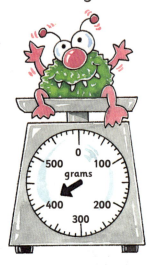

2 Jim the Giant's teeth weigh about ☐ kilograms.

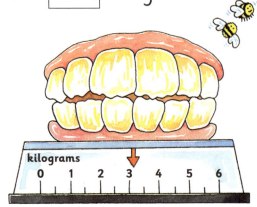

3 Sleepy the dwarf is about ☐ centimetres tall.

4 How tall are you? Find a tape measure and measure yourself.

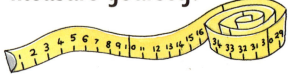

I'm about ☐ metre and ☐ centimetres tall.

Looking at kitchen scales and using a tape measure will help your child to learn more about measures. You can mark his height in pencil on a door and measure it again in a few months' time.

Fantastic!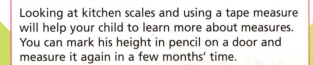

Choosing appropriate units for measuring

I'm 3 grams tall!

Imagine you are measuring these objects. Which measure would you use?

1

The drink for a giant could be measured in

....

2

The weight of a bus could be measured in

....

3

The length of a cat's whisker could be measured in

....

4

A drink for an elf in a thimble could be measured in

....

5

The distance from London to Glasgow could be measured in

....

6

The weight of a pirate's map could be measured in

....

 kilograms

centimetres

 metres

 grams

 kilometres

litres

 millilitres

Your child may well need lots of support working through this page as the concept of measuring different objects using different units is quite hard. Say *Your hand is small so we could measure it with a centimetre ruler. A giant's hand will be much bigger so we might need a metre ruler.*

Excellent!

Identifying true and untrue statements

Shape puzzles

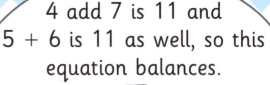

 4 add 7 is 11 and 5 + 6 is 11 as well, so this equation balances.

Tick ✓ the true number sentences.

Put a cross ✗ beside the untrue statements.

1) $4 + 7 = 5 + 6$ ✓   2) $10 + 10 = 99 + 1$

3) $2 \times 2 = 3$ 4) $100 + 1 = 101$

5) $27 + 33 = 30 + 30$ 6) $3 \times 3 = 8 + 2$

Now try these shape puzzles. Are they true or false?

true   false

7)  This shape has 5 sides and is called a hexagon.

8)  Half this rectangle is coloured red.

9) This is an equilateral triangle and the sides are all the same length.

Your child might find the calculations easier to check by covering up each sum in turn, working it out, then comparing the answers. Talk through the features of each shape with him before he ticks the true or false answer.

Lovely!

Interpreting a pictogram

Favourite stories

Penny Parrot chose four of her favourite stories. She then asked all the pirates which one they liked best. She drew this pictogram to show their answers.

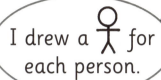
I drew a 👤 for each person.

Jim and the Beanstalk	👤 👤 👤 👤 👤
Kipper's Birthday	👤 👤 👤 👤
Winnie the Pooh	👤 👤
The Blue Balloon	👤 👤 👤 👤

1. How many pirates liked 'Winnie the Pooh'?

2. Which was the favourite book? ....

3. How many more pirates liked 'Jim and the Beanstalk' than liked 'Kipper's Birthday'?

4. How many pirates did Penny Parrot ask?

5. Write something else you can find out from the pictogram.

....

You could do this with your friends.

Discuss how the pictogram works before your child begins the activities. Talking about favourite books, and asking friends as well, will highlight how and why pictograms – and other graphs – are made.

Well done!

25

Solving problems with time

At Adventure Paradise

  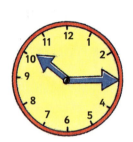

These clocks show hour, half hour and quarter hour times.

Work out the times Penny Parrot and her friend did things.

1. They get the bus at 8 o'clock. It takes half an hour to get to Adventure Paradise. Draw the hands on the clock to show the time they arrive.

2. The gates open at 9 o'clock.

   They have to wait ☐ minutes.

3. They go into the Model Village at 9.15am.

   If they come out at they spent ☐ minutes inside.

4. It is now 4.30pm. The bus goes home at 5.15pm. How many more minutes do they have in the park?

   ☐ minutes

Many children find telling the time difficult, so don't worry if your child still struggles with this. Make sure you have a clock available that is easy to read.

Wonderful!

Describing a route

Going home

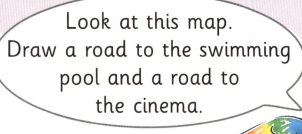
Look at this map. Draw a road to the swimming pool and a road to the cinema.

Imagine you are on the bus. Describe a route home. Tick each word as you use it!

forward ✓   turn left ☐   turn right ☐   go past ☐

Get on the bus and go forward. Turn ....

....

....

Remind your child to imagine that she is sitting on the bus, so that at the end of Rollercoaster Road she must turn right! Talk about your routes as you walk together to school or to the shops.

27

Working out two-step operations

Bus journeys

Work out how many people are on the bus by the end of each journey.

1  6 on the bus  2 off, 3 on  7 on the bus  1 off, 6 on  on the bus

2  5 on the bus  2 off, 1 on  on the bus  4 off, 2 on  on the bus

3  10 on the bus  3 off, 5 on  on the bus  none off, 6 on  on the bus

Now you choose the numbers.

4  on the bus  off, on  on the bus  off, on  on the bus

5  on the bus  off, on  on the bus  off, on  on the bus

Talk through the task before your child begins so he understand that he is keeping an on-going tally of the numbers of people. Make sure he doesn't rush the page as two-step operations are quite complex.

Brilliant!

Working out change

At the shop

You are going shopping for stationery. Work out what you spend each time, and how much change you get.

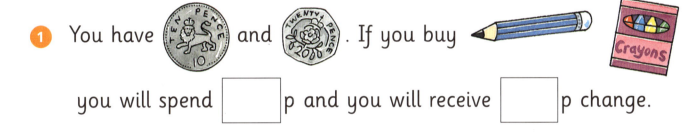

1. You have [10p coin] and [20p coin]. If you buy [pencil] [crayons] you will spend ☐ p and you will receive ☐ p change.

2. You have [50p coin]. If you buy [ruler] you will spend ☐ p and you will receive ☐ p change.

3. You have [£1 coin]. Do you have enough money to buy one of everything in the shop?

Real money could help to work the values out, but the numbers are small enough to encourage mental calculation. Encourage the use of pencil jottings to show how Question 3 is worked out.

Excellent!

29

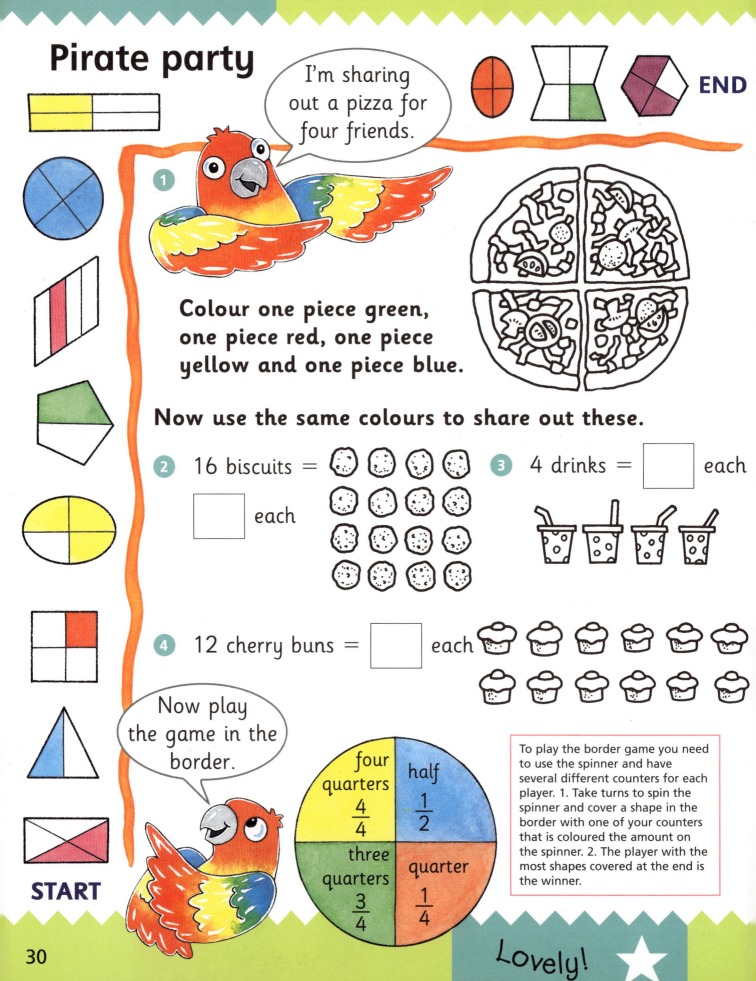

Revision

See what I can do

Circle the correct answer.

1. 2 quarters is the same as — a half / 3 quarters

2. 4 quarters is the same as — a half / a whole one

3. You measure orange juice in ....

4. A 3-sided shape is called a ....

5. The time on this clock is

   ....

6. 47 rounded to the nearest 10 is ☐

7. The even numbers from 2 to 12 in order, smallest first, are: ☐ ☐ ☐ ☐ ☐ ☐

8. £1.50 add £2 is £ ☐ . ☐

9. 78 splits into ▱ + ▱

10. 24 + 25 = ☐   11. 19 − 6 = ☐

I found 100 bees.

Yes   Almost

This page is to encourage your child by showing how much has been learned.

Great!

Answers

Pages 2–3
There are 11 trees, 17 coconuts, 14 sandcastles, 8 pirates, 18 fish, 12 sharks, 9 parrots (not including Penny), 20 coins.

Page 4
1) 12, 15, 18, 21   2) 20, 25, 30, 35
3) 6, 8, 10, 12, [14], 16, 18 – all even numbers
4) 11, [13, 15], 17   5) 4, [8, 16], 32 each number is double the last one

Page 5
1) 7, 8, 10, 12
2) 17, 24, 28, 39, 68, 86
3) 12, 14, 17, 21, 71, 96
4) 96, 64, 31, 17, 13, 12

Page 6
1) 5, 15, 20   2) 10, 30, 40, 60, 70, 90
3) 40, 55, 70, 85
4)

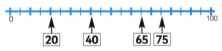

Page 7
1 and 2) check your child has completed the hundred square correctly.
3) 30   4) 80   5) 95   6) 49

Page 8
1) 263 = 200 + 60 + 3, 36 = 30 + 6, 487 = four hundred and eighty-seven, 79 = seventy-nine, 57 = 50 + 7, 300 = three hundred, 145 = 100 + 40 + 5
2) 68 = 60 + 8 = sixty-eight
3) 39 = 30 + 9 = thirty-nine
4) 46 = 40 + 6 = forty-six

Page 9
1) 100 + 20 + 3 = 123   2) check your child has added their score correctly
3) 600   4) 6 (or 0 if you miss the target!)

Page 10
1) 20   2) 40   3) 15 – 1 = 14   4) 15

Page 11
1) 11 – 3   2) 6 + 1   3) 18 – 1
4) 50 – 25   5) 3 + 13

Page 12
1) 13
2)

+	2	3	4	5	6	7
2	4	5	6	7	8	9
4	6	7	8	9	10	11
6	8	9	10	11	12	13
8	10	11	12	13	14	15
10	12	13	14	15	16	17

3)

+	5	8	10	7	11	0
10	15	18	20	17	21	10
20	25	28	30	27	31	20
25	30	33	35	32	36	25
30	35	38	40	37	41	30

Page 13
1) 18   2) 15   5) 10   6) 8   7) 23

Page 14
1) 12 stars, or about 10
2) 52 snowflakes, or about 50

Page 15
1) 40   2) 30   3) 90   4) 60   5) 20
6) 40

Pages 16–17
1) 46p   2) £1.16   3) £1.55
4) £1.40   5) £3.56   6) check your child has joined the correct values

Pages 18–19
2) 2cm deep and 4cm wide   3) 7cm
4) 9cm   5) 4cm   6) 4cm   7) 20cm
8) 10cm   9) 7cm   10) 10cm

Page 20
1) in order the shapes are cone, sphere, cuboid, cube, cylinder, pyramid   2) 6   3) 5   4) 3   5) 2
6) 5   7) 7

Page 21
Answers will vary, but check that they make sense.

Page 22
1) 400g   2) about 3kg
3) about 60cm

Page 23
1) litres   2) kilograms
3) centimetres   4) millilitres
5) kilometres   6) grams

Page 24
1) true   2) false   3) false   4) true
5) true   6) false   7) false   8) true
9) true

Page 25
1) 2   2) Jim and the Beanstalk
3) 1   4) 15   5) Answers will vary

Page 26
1) The hands should point at half past 8   2) 30 minutes   3) 15 minutes
4) 45 minutes

Page 28
1) 12   2) 4, 2   3) 12, 18

Page 29
1) 25p with 5p change   2) 27p and 23p change   3) No, you need £1.08

Page 30
2) 4 biscuits each   3) 1 drink each
4) 3 buns each

Page 31
1) a half   2) a whole one
3) litres or millilitres   4) triangle
5) half past 4 or 4.30   6) 50
7) 2, 4, 6, 8, 10, 12   8) £3.50
9) 70 + 8   10) 49   11) 13